# THE LITTLE GUIDE TO
# GIVENCHY

First published in 2025 by OH
An Imprint of HEADLINE PUBLISHING GROUP LIMITED

1

**Disclaimer:**

This book has not been licensed, approved, sponsored, or endorsed by Givenchy or any rightsholder(s) in respect of this brand.

Givenchy is a registered trademark owned by LVMH FRAGRANCE BRANDS and Givenchy S.A. (France)

Cataloguing in Publication Data is available from the British Library

ISBN 978-1-03542-276-0

Compiled and written by: Katie Meegan
Editorial: Saneaah Muhammad
Designed and typeset in Avenir by: Tony Seddon
Project manager: Russell Porter
Production: Arlene Lestrade
Printed and bound in Dubai

Headline's policy is to use papers that are natural, renewable and recyclable products and made from wood grown in well-managed forests and other controlled sources. The logging and manufacturing processes are expected to conform to the environmental regulations of the country of origin.

HEADLINE PUBLISHING GROUP LIMITED
An Hachette UK Company
Carmelite House, 50 Victoria Embankment, London EC4Y 0DZ

The authorised representative in the EEA is Hachette Ireland, 8 Castlecourt Centre, Dublin 15, D15 XTP3, Ireland (email: info@hbgi.ie)

www.headline.co.uk    www.hachette.co.uk

THE LITTLE GUIDE TO

# GIVENCHY

STYLE TO LIVE BY

Unofficial and Unauthorized

# CONTENTS

# INTRODUCTION

The House of Givenchy is both rooted in cultural history and unabashedly modern. Givenchy is timeless Parisian chic, but it is also New York street style. It is haute couture and wearable elegance. And therein the many contradictions of Givenchy lies its inherent genius – the ability to make the wearer feel like a 50s Hollywood starlet, a gothic fantasy figure or a 90s supermodel.

The House of Givenchy, and the direction of modern fashion, is all down to the vision of one man – Hubert de Givenchy. A member of the French nobility, Givenchy stood at an eye-catching six foot six, renowned for his aristocratic charm and eye for detail. From his early years in post-war Paris, guided by renowned mentors such as Cristóbal Balenciaga, to his mastery of fabrics and finishes, Givenchy's work exemplified elegance and sophistication.

Central to the legacy of Givenchy was Hubert's lifelong friendship with Audrey Hepburn, whose iconic looks on and off the screen helped define the refined, minimalist aesthetic that is synonymous with the fashion house. Some of the most recognizable and iconic designs of the twentieth century were born from this collaboration, not only the *Breakfast at Tiffany's* little black dress but also the *Sabrina* neckline and the many costumes of *Funny Face*.

Hubert de Givenchy remained head of his fashion house until his retirement in 1995. Having had such a steady and clear creative direction for so long under its eponymous designer, the House of Givenchy without Hubert took several years to find its new voice. Givenchy continued to evolve under contemporary creative directions, adapting the founder's timeless vision for modern generations while honouring his legacy. As fashion moved into the twenty-first century, Givenchy's successors have sought to balance innovation with the elegance and sophistication that defined the brand's origins.

However, one thing remains for sure: The legacy of Hubert de Givenchy, master of elegance, refinement and luxury.

# CHAPTER ONE

# THE EARLY YEARS AND MENTORS

BORN INTO THE FRENCH ARISTOCRACY, HUBERT DE GIVENCHY WAS DESTINED FOR CREATIVE GREATNESS FROM AN EARLY AGE. HOWEVER, IT WAS THE MENTORS THAT HE MET ALONG THE WAY THAT REALLY CATAPULTED HIM TO THE HEIGHTS OF COUTURE.

Count Hubert James Marcel Taffin de Givenchy was born on February 20, 1927, to a family of French nobility.

The youngest son of Lucien Taffin de Givenchy, Marquis of Givenchy, and his wife Béatrice, Hubert had one older brother and a sister who died in infancy.

It was always my dream to be a dress designer, and my mother accepted that decision.

**Givenchy**

On his lifelong dream of becoming a fashion designer, nytimes.com, March 12, 2018

To do my job and strive to do my best: Something that I learned from my mother. All my life I have tried to forge my own path and follow it.

**Givenchy**

On the influence of his mother on his creative life, system-magazine.com, 2015

I'd love to wear the big pant, like I see on the street… but I'd look ridiculous. I'm not that shape.

## Givenchy

Famously, Givenchy was a very tall man, standing at an eye-catching six foot six inches, wwd.com, original article published June 12, 1978

**"**

Hubert de Givenchy is one of only a handful of fashion designers who have changed the way women feel about themselves, their bodies and the clothes they wear.

**"**

**Karen Homer**

*Little Book of Givenchy*, Karen Homer, 2023

I always draw when I have the desire to or when I feel inspired.

**Givenchy**

On his creative upbringing, system-magazine.com, 2015

Hubert de Givenchy's father passed away suddenly from influenza when he was still a young child. This meant that he was raised by his mother and aunts.

He would later cite this strong feminine influence in his early life as pivotal to his understanding of design for women.

My mother was a beautiful lady, elegant, chic, and that was the biggest inspiration to me.

**Givenchy**

On the first person to inspire him – his mother, graciousquotes.com, December 1, 2023

Artistic professions ran in the Givenchy family.

Hubert's maternal grandfather owned a tapestry manufacturer and his great-grandfather was a set designer at the Paris Opera.

You must respect yourself.

**Givenchy**

On self-reflection, wwd.com, original article published June 12, 1978

> [Designs] were displayed in a show as smoothly elegant as the most experienced house in Paris could put on – in quarters so cramped that ironing was done in the bathroom.

**_Life_ magazine**

On Givenchy's 1952 debut show, nytimes.com, March 12, 2018

Fabric is the most extraordinary thing, it has life. You must respect the fabric.

**Givenchy**

On his love of fine fabrics – solidified after a visit to the 1937 World's Fair in Paris, independent.co.uk, June 7, 2010

It was just after the war. Entering the world of fashion was another way of trying to forget the difficult years that we'd been through.

## Givenchy

Recalling the precarious position that the French fashion scene was left in following the devastation of World War II, system-magazine.com, 2015

With the support of his mother and older brother, Hubert moved to Paris at the age of 17, where he enrolled at the influential art school, École des Beaux-Arts.

At the time, Paris was still under Nazi occupation.

The more pretty you look, the
more love affairs you will have.

**Givenchy**

Sharing words of wisdom, independent.co.uk, June 7, 2010

Givenchy's first designs were created during his apprenticeships with the influential fashion designers Jacques Fath, Robert Piguet and Lucien Lelong, where he worked alongside Christian Dior and Pierre Balmain.

From 1947 to 1951, Givenchy worked in the atelier of the avant-garde revolutionary designer Elsa Schiaparelli.

People say I am a classic designer.
I don't try to be classic, but I do try
to be simple and elegant.

**Givenchy**

On his personal style as a designer, graciousquotes.com,
December 1, 2023

> **"**
>
> Hubert didn't make any mistake in his choices. Schiaparelli – at the very start of his career path – illuminated [him with her] creative and contagious genius… linked to the poetic movements of her time, illuminated by freedom.
>
> **"**

**Emanuel Ungaro**

French fashion designer, on Schiaparelli's influence on Givenchy, wwd.com, March 13, 2018

A haven of fun and fantasy… the atmosphere completely captivated me. Entering Jacques Fath's fashion house was like stepping into a universe of danger and sensuality.

### Givenchy

On his traineeship with legendary designer Jacques Fath, *Little Book of Givenchy*, Karen Homer, 2023

In 1952, aged 25, Givenchy opened his own design atelier.

He caught the attention of the fashion press for his innovative use of separates and designs featuring particularly cheap materials, such as linen.

When I began to be a designer,
I remember Hattie Carnegie came
and ordered 18 pieces.
Ben Zuckerman was there and many
American buyers… That whole
atmosphere of couture.

**Givenchy**

On the influx of American clientele into the European fashion
centres of Paris and Milan post World War II, wwd.com, originally
published June 12, 1978

Applause at his premiere was loud, unqualified and long.

**American *Vogue***

On Givenchy's first solo show, *Little Book of Givenchy,*
Karen Homer, 2023

My ambition was to become an assistant in a couture house and to become a couturier myself.

**Givenchy**

On his youthful ambitions, system-magazine.com, 2015

1953 was a pivotal year for Hubert de Givenchy.

It was during this year that he would meet two people who would alter the course of his life, fashion house and, ultimately, the way that we dress to this day: Cristóbal Balenciaga and Audrey Hepburn.

# CHAPTER TWO

# MATERIALS AND MUSES

HUBERT DE GIVENCHY'S GENTLEMANLY CHARM QUICKLY ENDEARED HIM TO SOME OF THE MOST POWERFUL AND INFLUENTIAL WOMEN IN THE TWENTIETH CENTURY.

COMBINED WITH HIS PASSION FOR FINE MATERIAL AND DESIGN, AND UNDER THE STEWARDSHIP OF CRISTÓBAL BALENCIAGA, HE WAS SOON CATAPULTED TO THE TOP OF THE PARISIAN FASHION SCENE.

I love to drive my car (an old Mercedes) and be the first in my couture house. I adore that. Perhaps I'm masochistic. But I'm so happy to have this big house. I wait for my secretary, the models. If they need me, I'll stay late at night. But I'm an early morning man.

**Givenchy**

On his daily routine as head of a renowned fashion house, wwd.com, originally published June 12, 1978

Hubert de Givenchy was renowned for dressing some of the most aesthetically and culturally influential women of the twentieth century.

His first collection was named "Bettina Graziani", after one of the world's first supermodels; a French woman who walked for him and was his early muse.

It was an immense pleasure to work with these extraordinary personalities, and I had different experiences working with each of these legendary women.

### Givenchy

Always speaking highly of the clientele he designed for,
system-magazine.com, 2015

Other influential women that Givenchy dressed included Ingrid Bergman, Greta Garbo, Gloria Guinness and Jacqueline Kennedy Onassis.

I met Mrs Kennedy. She loved what I was doing and she trusted me. When she became the First Lady of the United States, her feelings remained unchanged and we often worked together…
Mrs Kennedy simply picked out dresses from the collection.

**Givenchy**

On working with the former first lady Jacqueline Kennedy, system-magazine.com, 2015

The General said to me, 'Madame, this afternoon you look like a real Parisian.'

**Jacqueline Kennedy**

Dressed by Givenchy, Jacqueline Kennedy recalled being complimented by General Charles de Gaulle, lofficielph.com, February 20, 2021

Everything from his own debut, in embroidered cotton, his fresh-spirited approach to couture, so French with a mixture of simplicity and a zip of daringness.

**Christian Lacroix**

Fellow designer, on the ground-breaking nature of Givenchy's first collection, wwd.com, March 13, 2018

You'd see a goddess, the image of that lady. You'd be thinking of a large private ballroom with her in it.

**Givenchy**

On socialite, editor and fashion icon Gloria Guinness, one of the many famous women he dressed, wwd.com, originally published June 12, 1978

> Those stiff, cut-out little Givenchy coats couldn't give a damn. The coat was so sharp and brittle and so positive it was right. Not that the women were arrogant. The clothes made them arrogant.

**William J. Cunningham**

A rather interesting take on Givenchy by the *Women's Wear Daily* columnist, *Vintage Handbags: Collecting and Wearing Vintage Classics*, Marnie Fogg, 2022

[The clothes of Calvin Klein have a] linear simplicity [and Yves Saint Laurent] completely understands his epoch. [I create] a product in good taste – that is perhaps classic and well made.

**Givenchy**

Sharing who he admired among the next generation of fashion designers from the 1970s, wwd.com, originally published June 12, 1978

I must say Cristóbal Balenciaga.

**Givenchy**

On his greatest influence, system-magazine.com, 2015

In 1953, Givenchy met Cristóbal Balenciaga. While he never officially worked under the Spanish designer, Balenciaga became a mentor and guide to Givenchy, influencing him in many areas of design and business.

So much so that Givenchy even moved his design studio to be closer to Balenciaga's.

I admired the work of Balenciaga and, of course, that of other couturiers. I was already very selective.

**Givenchy**

On being drawn to Balenciaga, system-magazine.com, 2015

Givenchy was inspired by Balenciaga's take on shape and ready-to-wear collection that debuted in 1954.

Critics enjoyed the loose style of dresses that were both comfortable and chic.

[A garment by Balenciaga] is like a surgery – by technique, it gives to women with bad posture some allure.

**Givenchy**

Finding inspiration in Balenciaga's keen attention to details and fluid lines, incorporating these ideals into his own designs, wwd.com, originally published June 12, 1978

Balenciaga was my religion.
Since I'm a believer, for me, there's
Balenciaga, and the good Lord.

### Givenchy

On his passion for Balenciaga, nytimes.com, March 12, 2018

He was devoted to his master Balenciaga, but had his own touch.

## Christian Lacroix

Designer Christian Lacroix, on the lessons that Givenchy took from Balenciaga, wwd.com, March 13, 2018

I was in awe of him. I was fascinated by his meticulousness. He knew how to do everything – cut a dress, assemble it from a pattern. He had worked in London and elsewhere, and had forged his own vision of fashion through which he was able to express his creativity. He allowed me to prove myself and to develop my own ideas and creativity.

**Givenchy**

Crediting his relationship with Balenciaga as a positive force in his creative life, system-magazine.com, 2015

**"**

His encounter with Cristóbal Balenciaga was decisive in the architecture of his creativity, [and he retained] the major lessons of this genius.

**"**

**Emmanuel Ungaro**

French designer, on Balenciaga's influence on Givenchy, wwd.com, March 13, 2018

His exceptional work, his extraordinary career, his creativity, his values and above all, his elegance. When I first met him, I was influenced by his self-belief, his refusal to cheat, his simplicity and his honesty.

## Givenchy

Praising the man he called his "master" – Givenchy and Balenciaga were a pair that changed the fashion world forever, system-magazine.com, 2015

Givenchy and Balenciaga remained close friends until the latter's death in 1977. In 2011, the Cristóbal Balenciaga Museum opened in his hometown of Getaria, Spain.

Not only was Givenchy in attendance, but Balenciaga's museum itself was made possible by the donation of many pieces from his former mentee.

All the proportions of Balenciaga are strong, modern, wonderful.

**Givenchy**

On his mentor and muse Balenciaga, independent.co.uk, June 7, 2010

Givenchy is credited with introducing the shift dress in 1955, and later the 1957 sac dress, also called the "Chemise" dress.

This shape then inspired Christian Dior's 1957 Fuseau/Spindle line.

In every moment you must
be attentive and notice the little
things to be creative.

**Givenchy**

On creativity, independent.co.uk, June 7, 2010

Luxury is in each detail.

**Givenchy**

graciousquotes.com, December 1, 2023

Other iconic designs that Givenchy is credited with inventing are the "Balloon" coat, the "Baby Doll" dress in 1958 and the "Princess Line" dress in 1959.

[Givenchy] was one of the first to make the leap into ready-to-wear with very wearable fabrics and styles.

99

**Ralph Toledano**

President of the Fédération de la Haute Couture et de la Mode, on Givenchy's legacy, wwd.com, March 13, 2018

You are like a butterfly, in every moment you must have good reception.

**Givenchy**

On how to create timeless designs, independent.co.uk, June 7, 2010

# CHAPTER
## THREE

# THE SILVER SCREEN
# AND
# AUDREY HEPBURN

IT WOULD BE IMPOSSIBLE
TO TALK ABOUT THE CAREER OR
LIFE OF HUBERT DE GIVENCHY
WITHOUT MENTIONING THE
ICONIC AUDREY HEPBURN;
HIS MUSE, CHAMPION AND
LIFE-LONG FRIEND.

TOGETHER, GIVENCHY
AND HEPBURN CREATED A NEW
LANGUAGE OF ELEGANCE.

66

She wore tight little pants and a little T-shirt, and I was so disappointed she wasn't Katharine. I said I had no time – I was in the middle of making my second collection, and I didn't have too many workers then. But we had dinner that night, and before dinner was over, I told her, 'I'll do anything for you.'

99

### Givenchy

Sharing the story of his first meeting with Audrey Hepburn – an anecdote often repeated, nytimes.com, March 12, 2018

In 1953, Hubert de Givenchy met Audrey Hepburn. At first, he did not know who the starlet was, assuming that he was meeting the established actress Katharine Hepburn.

However, after one meeting, a deep friendship and connection between Audrey and Hubert was born.

All a woman needs to be chic is a raincoat, two suits, a pair of trousers and a cashmere sweater.

**Givenchy**

On women's essential fashion, graciousquotes.com, December 1, 2023

[Givenchy and Hepburn] invented the icon of a certain Parisienne.

**Christian Lacroix**

Fellow French designer, on Givenchy and Hepburn's influence on the fashion world, wwd.com, March 13, 2018

From that day on, until she died – too early for me – the friendship was really like a special love affair.

**Givenchy**

On his lifelong friendship with Audrey Hepburn,
independent.co.uk, June 7, 2010

**"**

When I first went to Hubert, I was still in homemade dresses.

**"**

## Audrey Hepburn

The iconic actress telling *Vogue* about how Givenchy instantly elevated her style, nytimes.com, March 12, 2018

Fresh, unique, loyal, wonderful.

## Givenchy

Describing his friend and muse Audrey Hepburn in four words, independent.co.uk, June 7, 2010

*Sabrina* (1954), starring Audrey Hepburn, was the first film that Givenchy designed costumes for.

Givenchy created what then became known as the Sabrina (or bateau) neckline – a wide neckline that runs horizontally, front and back, almost to the shoulder points, across the collarbone.

Audrey was someone who knew perfectly how to dress, and knew perfectly what she should wear. What counted was her eyes, her face and her silhouette. We refined, purified, cleared away for her face. We had to, as I would say, surround Audrey. The results were extraordinary because her face and her style became my style.

## Givenchy

Telling *The New York Times* in 2018 about his design ethos concerning Audrey Hepburn, wmagazine.com, July 1, 2018

However, not all were happy about the partnership between Givenchy and Hepburn. In the 1950s, it was rare for Hollywood studios to use designs from outside sources.

The head of costume of Universal at the time was Edith Head, who took full credit for Givenchy's designs when winning the Oscar for costume design for *Sabrina*.

With her, work became an act of joy.

**Givenchy**

On working with Audrey Hepburn, system-magazine.com, 2015

His are the only clothes in which I am myself. He is far more than a couturier. He is a creator of personality.

**Audrey Hepburn**

On her good friend Givenchy, wmagazine.com,
July 1, 2018

I absolutely believe my talent is God-given. I ask God for a lot, but I also thank him. I'm a very demanding believer.

**Givenchy**

On his innate talents in fashion, graciousquotes.com, December 1, 2023

Each time I'm in a film, Givenchy dresses me.

**Audrey Hepburn**

Clarifying to the world that it was Givenchy's designs that she wore, nytimes.com, March 12, 2018

However, film studio pushback didn't prevent Givenchy and Hepburn from working together.

In 1961, Givenchy designed one of the most iconic dresses of the twentieth century – the *Breakfast at Tiffany's* little black dress.

The little black dress is the hardest thing to realize, because you must keep it simple.

**Givenchy**

On the iconic *Breakfast at Tiffany's* little black dress, nytimes.com, March 12, 2018

It's a good silhouette – and it's still the same... That long neck, the long legs, the charming face... Of course, she's not 20 anymore. But the allure and the silhouette, they're still the same.

### Givenchy

Speaking in 1978, on Audrey Hepburn's timeless elegance, wwd.com, originally published June 12, 1978

The legendary *Breakfast at Tiffany's* dress was sold in 2006 at a charity auction to a private buyer.

Estimated to be worth between £50,000 and £70,000, in the end it fetched an astounding £467,200 ($920,000).

The change from the little girl who arrived that morning was unbelievable. The way she moved in the suit, she was so happy. She said that it was exactly what she wanted for the movie. She gave a life to the clothes.

**Givenchy**

On the sophistication that his clothes provided for Audrey Hepburn, *Little Book of Givenchy*, Karen Homer, 2023

"

From the front, the dress was simple enough: sleek and sleeveless with a flattering bateau neckline. From the back, it was dynamic, sexy and utterly sophisticated with its geometric cutouts and the alluring way it framed the nape of the neck.

"

**The Washington Post**

On the timeless allure of the *Breakfast at Tiffany's* dress, washingtonpost.com, March 12, 2018

We have a wonderful camaraderie.

## Givenchy

Speaking to British Vogue about the relationship with his friend
and muse, Audrey Hepburn, bfi.org.uk, August 4, 2015

**"**

Givenchy's creations always gave me a sense of security and confidence and my work went more easily in the knowledge that I looked absolutely right. I felt the same at my private appearances. Givenchy's outfits gave me 'protection' against strange situations and people. I felt so good in them.

**"**

## Audrey Hepburn

On using Givenchy's designs as a form of armour against the world, thecut.com, April 3, 2016

The partnership between Givenchy and Hepburn also bred the first celebrity-inspired perfume.

The legend goes that Givenchy created the fragrance in 1954 as a present for Hepburn, who then "forbade" him from selling it anywhere else – hence the name "L'Interdit".

Eventually the star relented and even became the face of the perfume.

Mine is one of the most beautiful professions in fashion: making others happy with an idea.

**Givenchy**

On his place in fashion, wwd.com, March 13, 2018

In advertising the L'Interdit perfume, Hepburn became the first celebrity "face" to endorse a perfume, setting into motion the trend for celebrity-endorsed perfumes that continues to this day.

Hepburn even wore the perfume during the filming of *Paris When It Sizzles* (1964), ensuring that Givenchy received a screen credit for it.

You must, if it's possible, be born with a kind of elegance. It's part of you, of yourself.

## Givenchy

His advice when speaking to a graduation class of designers in 2010, nytimes.com, March 12, 2018

# Films starring Audrey Hepburn and costumed by Givenchy – look out for the following:

### *Sabrina* (1954)

The white strapless ball gown, similar to Hepburn's 1954 Academy Awards dress when she won an Oscar for Best Actress.

### *Funny Face* (1957)

The bridal dress, which is shorter than expected, with netting for a puffed-out effect, a high, scooped neckline and capped sleeves.

### *Love in the Afternoon* (1957)

The white point d'espirit ball gown, which she wears to the opera, highlighted with a detailed trim and bow at the waist.

### *Breakfast at Tiffany's* (1961)

Loved by movie goers and fashion followers the world over, the iconic little black cocktail dress that defined Hepburn's career, and a style that continues to inspire to this day.

### *Charade* (1963)
High-buttoned jackets, coats and raincoats, sleek pencil skirts and shift dresses, all complete with accessories, highlighted by Hepburn's red suit and pillbox hat as she walks alongside the Seine.

### *Paris When It Sizzles* (1964)
A collection of elegant two-piece suits and shift dresses.

### *How to Steal a Million* (1966)
Classic 1960s style clothes with Audrey making a memorable entrance in an all-white ensemble of jacket and skirt with large white-rimmed glasses and white pillbox hat.

### *Love Among Thieves* (1987)
The film harks back to Givenchy's costumes from his previous designs, most noticeably a red dress that recalls the one Hepburn wore in *Funny Face*.

Hepburn and Givenchy remained firm friends throughout both of their lives and remain one of the most famous fashion friendships to this day.

When the telephone would ring in the studio, I knew when it was her. I would answer and she'd say, 'I know you are busy, but I just want to send you a big kiss,' and she'd hang up. That was Audrey.

**Givenchy**

Remembering his friend, muse and "sister" Audrey Hepburn, nytimes.com, March 15, 2018

# CHAPTER FOUR

# THE ART
# OF ELEGANCE

A CHAMPION OF WOMEN,
GIVENCHY WAS THE VERY ESSENCE
OF TIMELESS ELEGANCE, COMFORT
AND SOPHISTICATED STYLE.

THROUGHOUT THE SECOND HALF
OF THE TWENTIETH CENTURY,
HUBERT DE GIVENCHY REMAINED A
STALWART OF THE HAUTE COUTURE
SCENE, EXPANDING HIS EMPIRE
INTO READY-TO-WEAR, MENSWEAR,
ACCESSORIES AND EVEN CARS.

I like to make beautiful things, to feel them in my hands. But I also love the pleasure of seeing a dress come alive on a woman. It's a short-lived sensation, but there is nothing like it.

**Givenchy**

On creating beautiful fashion, wwd.com, March 13, 2018

The House of Givenchy went from strength to strength throughout the 1960s.

In 1968, Givenchy opened its first ready-to-wear luxury store in Paris, and in 1969, Givenchy launched his menswear collection named "Gentleman Givenchy".

## The dress must follow the woman's body, not the body after the dress.

**Givenchy**

He was a champion of women, creating clothing to suit the shape of the person he was designing for, not forcing them into showpieces, lofficielph.com, February 20, 2021

He always respected the woman's body, never inflicting what was cool but only what was flattering.

**Valentino Garavani**

Fellow designer Valentino Garavani praises Givenchy for his dedication to dressing the woman over the trend, wwd.com, March 13, 2018

Everything is so difficult now. One season there are broad shoulders, then none at all. A short dress, then a long dress. There's no continuity. To change just because of change, that is not my idea at all.

**Givenchy**

Speaking in 1978, bemoaning the seasonality of fashion, wwd.com, originally published June 12, 1978

What fires his imagination races hers. The message he cuts into cloth she beams into the world with the special wit and stylishness of a great star.

**American _Vogue_**

On the unique collaboration between Givenchy and Hepburn, bfi.org.uk, August 4, 2015

"

He was pure elegance.

"

**Daphne Guinness**

Fellow designer, on Givenchy, wwd.com, originally published
June 12, 1978

It's the loyal customers who will always buy. You wouldn't believe how many Swiss and German and English women spend money. **"**

## Givenchy

On his ideal clientele, wwd.com, originally published June 12, 1978

**"**

It was so innate in him. I think there was nothing that went by unnoticed for him with regard to a woman: her carriage, her manner of dress and, maybe most importantly, if what she wore made her feel confident.

**"**

## Gabriella de Givenchy

Great-niece to the designer Gabriella de Givenchy remembers Givenchy's ability to tap into what his client needed, wmagazine.com, July 1, 2018

For me, haute couture is everything.

## Givenchy

In conversation with Claire Waight Keller, the first woman to be creative director of the house, wwd.com, March 13, 2018

Throughout the 1970s, Givenchy continued to expand into shoes, jewellery, homeware, interiors and even into cars, designing the interior of the Continental Mark V towncar.

There's a place for all that – the trendy things. You need a spot for everybody.

**Givenchy**

Acknowledging the role of trend-led fashion, wwd.com, originally published June 12, 1978

You must adapt.

**Givenchy**

On keeping up with the times in 1978, wwd.com, originally published June 12, 1978

**"**

His daytime clothes are calm
and satisfying, his evening grand
and beautiful. He epitomizes the
best in fashion – controlled, classic,
luminous.

**"**

## Bernadine Morris

Fashion critic and buyer Bernadine Morris on Givenchy's designs,
cdfa.com, March 12, 2018

To be a couture designer is not only to create dresses but to adapt your line to your private customers. It is why couture is expensive. You are like a doctor.

**Givenchy**

On the meticulousness of designing for private clients, graciousquotes.com, December 1, 2023

Well, for one thing, it gives
Givenchy a night off.

## Simon Dermott

Played by Peter O'Toole, the character makes the tongue-in-cheek
reference when Hepburn, who plays an art collector's daughter,
dons a maid's outfit as a disguise in *How to Steal a Million* (1966),
imbd.com

Mr Givenchy was a man of flawless taste and style, he created an incredible legacy of elegance, beauty and timeless perfection and was a global inspiration that went beyond fashion and film.

**Julien MacDonald**

Designer Julien MacDonald, who served as creative director of Givenchy for two years from 2002–2004, wwd.com, March 13, 2018

Everyone wants to have the liberty
to wear anything, everything.

**Givenchy**

wwd.com, originally published June 12, 1978

The ability of the designer to create his life according to his desire never changes.

"

**Givenchy**

On the life of a designer, system-magazine.com, 2015

He was an icon, not only of fashion, but of style. He was just elegant in everything he did.

**Marco Gobbetti**

Luxury businessman Marco Gobbetti on Givenchy's legacy, wwd.com, March 13, 2018

[Women today] want as little
as possible in their wardrobes that
would complicate their lives.

**Givenchy**

Credited with popularizing the capsule wardrobe, wwd.com,
originally published June 12, 1978

**"**

The perfect combination of elegance, savoir faire and creativity.

**"**

## Riccardo Tisci

Designer Riccardo Tisci, on the House of Givenchy, where he served as creative director for twelve years from 2005–2017, wwd.com, March 13, 2018

# CHAPTER
# FIVE

# SELLING UP AND SUCCESSION

IN ORDER TO COMPETE IN
THE EVER-CHANGING FASHION
LANDSCAPE, HUBERT DE GIVENCHY
SOLD HIS FASHION HOUSE TO
LVMH IN 1988.

AFTER HEADING UP THE HOUSE
OF GIVENCHY FOR NEARLY
FORTY YEARS, HE RETIRED FROM
FASHION IN 1995.

In 1988, luxury conglomerate LVMH bought the House of Givenchy. This move came two years after the sale of Givenchy's perfume division to LVMH. As part of the deal, Hubert de Givenchy remained head of design until his retirement in 1995.

I am of tradition, but that doesn't mean I have an old outlook on life.

**Givenchy**

On combining tradition and innovation, wwd.com, originally published June 12, 1978

It's always difficult for a designer when they move away from their brand, there's always this strong emotional attachment, and he demonstrated that and spoke to me about it. The good news for him is his brand's still alive, his name's still alive. I think that's a great thing.

**Ozwald Boateng**

Saville Row tailor who was head of Givenchy menswear from 2004–2007, wwd.com, March 13, 2018

66

There are few careers in fashion
like Hubert de Givenchy.

99

**Philippe Venet**

Givenchy's partner for more than six decades, lofficielph.com,
February 20, 2021

No, I no longer look at fashion. The world is a very different place now. I sometimes ask myself, 'Has elegance disappeared? Is there no longer any direction in contemporary fashion?' It all makes very little sense to me.

**Givenchy**

Criticizing the disappearance of elegance, system-magazine.com, 2015

> " In both prestigious long dresses and daywear, Hubert de Givenchy has brought together two rare qualities: to be innovative and timeless. "

**Bernard Arnault**

Chairman and chief executive officer of LVMH (Louis Vuitton Moët Hennessy), wwd.com, March 13, 2018

127

Every epoch is different, and you must accept the reality. C'est la vie.

**Givenchy**

On the reality of fashion designers, independent.co.uk, June 7, 2010

Givenchy's accolades included the Chevalier de la Légion d'Honneur in 1983 and a lifetime achievement award from the Council of Fashion Designers of America in 1995.

It's another feeling. It's a difficult thing not to have a nostalgia for the beginning of my career. At that time is was very encouraging to be a designer. In two days you'd cover all the money you spend to make a collection – that's something to be nostalgic about.

**Givenchy**

Reminiscing on the heyday of haute couture, wwd.com, originally published June 12, 1978

The emotion at Hubert de Givenchy's final fashion show was palpable.

In a touching gesture, Givenchy invited the staff of his atelier to take a final bow alongside him on the catwalk for the final time.

Happily, for many years we had a wonderful time. Beautiful fabric, beautiful people, beautiful memories.

**Givenchy**

From his retirement speech in 1995, independent.co.uk, June 7, 2010

**"**

Hubert Givenchy was the true gentleman of fashion… He brought such integrity to the world of design and though we will miss the man, his spirit will continue to inspire us.

**"**

**Ralph Lauren**

Fashion designer, on the legacy of Givenchy, wwd.com, March 13, 2018

Those in attendance to honour Givenchy's last show included fellow designers Yves Saint Laurent, Christian Lacroix and Oscar de la Renta.

" What I found extraordinary was not so much his longevity as the way he managed to withdraw completely from fashion to enter a totally different field and have two separate careers. It's very interesting and very impressive. "

**Ralph Toledano**

President of the Fédération de la Haute Couture et de la Mode, on Givenchy's work in the world of fine art and auctioneering, wwd.com, March 13, 2018

Upon his retirement from fashion, Givenchy continued to work with international auction house Christie's, as chairman of the international supervisory board.

I think when you sell your company, and are no longer the master of driving it, it's quite difficult… I don't think I have any interest any more. It's better like that.

**Givenchy**

On retirement, independent.co.uk, June 7, 2010

I've stopped making clothes but not making discoveries. Life is like a book: one must know when it is time to turn the page.

**Givenchy**

On moving on from fashion, lofficielph.com, February 20, 2021

**"**

France has lost a master. A master
of elegance, creation and invention,
a master of his culture and
ambassador of this spirit of liberty
and audacity.

**"**

**Emmanuel Macron**

French President Emmanuel Macron, on Givenchy,
wwd.com, March 13, 2018

Hubert de Givenchy passed away peacefully in his sleep on March 10, 2018, in Neuilly-sur-Seine, France, at the age of 91.

A visionary in the world of fashion, his legacy of elegance and timeless design continues to inspire generations.

66

He was a fundamental inspiration for my work in my entire life – a true friend and the grandest gentleman I have ever met in my life, a wonderful man and living expression of class, style and taste.

99

**Albert Kriemler**

Akris creative director, on his friend and inspiration Givenchy, wwd.com, March 13, 2018

# CHAPTER
# SIX

# GIVENCHY FOR A NEW CENTURY

SINCE GIVENCHY'S DEPARTURE FROM HIS EPONYMOUS FASHION HOUSE, A HOST OF DESIGNERS HAVE ATTEMPTED TO STEP INTO HIS SHOES AS CREATIVE DIRECTOR – ALL WITH VARYING DEGREES OF PRECEDING REPUTATION AND SUCCESS.

The day after Givenchy's retirement was confirmed, his replacement was announced – British designer to the stars and "enfant terrible" of the 1990s – John Galliano.

Creating at Givenchy, even briefly, pushed me to think of couture as not just clothing but as art.

**John Galliano**

On the lessons he learned during his time at Givenchy, globalfashionreport.com

I am a completely obsessive man.

**John Galliano**

On his success within the fashion world, newyorker.com,
September 14, 2003

"

But the sense that anyone could imagine this show is perhaps the problem; Mr Galliano was hired because he has a better imagination than most.

"

### *The New York Times*

A review of Galliano's first Givenchy show, nytimes.com, March 18, 1996

Galliano's first show at Givenchy was an abrupt departure from the refined elegance that the fashion house was known for.

The Spring/Summer 1996 collection received mixed reviews, and Galliano was soon replaced by fellow "bad boy" designer and Englishman, Alexander McQueen.

Why? It's very successful. It makes money from fashion and from perfumes.

**Bernard Arnault**

Owner of LVMH, when asked if he would close Givenchy
upon the retirement of the eponymous designer, nytimes.com,
March 25, 2001

I suffer. What is happening doesn't make me happy. After all, one is proud of one's name.

**Givenchy**

On his disappointment regarding how the House of Givenchy was managed after his retirement, nytimes.com, March 12, 2018

While balancing his own label, McQueen shocked the fashion world with the Autumn/Winter 1997 collection, which saw models clad in leopard print strut through a slaughterhouse.

The collection was a far cry from the elegant femininity of the original Givenchy, disturbing the house's loyal clientele, but was a hit with critics who appreciated McQueen's bold style.

I treated Givenchy badly. It was just money to me. But there was nothing I could do: the only way it would have worked would have been if they had allowed me to change the whole concept of the House, to give it a new identity, and they never wanted me to do that.

**Alexander McQueen**

On the mixed feelings he experienced during his time at Givenchy, haloscape.org, February 28, 2024

An old horse slaughterhouse on the edge of Paris, where cobblestone floors slanted toward drains for the flow of animal blood.

### *The New York Times*

On Alexander McQueen's 1997 debut Givenchy show, "Search for the Golden Fleece", nytimes.com, March 10, 2015

I am not intimidated by the exponents of Parisian haute couture. I am not afraid of them at all. I want to bring back that sophisticated ease that is unique to Givenchy, that's what I want to do. Staying true to myself, without a doubt.

**Alexander McQueen**

On the mix of high and low culture that he strived to bring to Givenchy, nssmag.com, August 8, 2024

> **"**
>
> Someone like him, coming from a working-class family, known for his crazy, iconoclastic creations, was chosen by one of the most prestigious Parisian maisons: All the English celebrated the event as if they had won the World Cup. **"**

**Ian Bonhôte**

Director of the documentary *Alexander McQueen: Il genio della moda (The genius of fashion)*, nssmag.com, August 8, 2024

Despite his obvious talent, McQueen's designs never fully aligned with the ethos of Givenchy.

After a series of controversial moves, one of which was selling a controlling stake of McQueen's own label to LVMH's rival, the Gucci Group, McQueen departed Givenchy in 2001 to focus on his own label.

I may be quite mad on the public circuit, but I've got my head screwed on – tight with a wrench.

**Alexander McQueen**

Speaking to *The Daily Telegraph* soon after his appointment to Givenchy, haloscape.org, February 28, 2024

Creative Directors of Givenchy
from 1995–present:

## John Galliano
### (1995–1996)
First show: Spring 1996 Couture Collection,
Paris, January 1996

## Alexander McQueen
### (1996–2001)
First show: "Search for the Golden Fleece" Spring
1997 Couture Collection, Paris, January 1997

## Julien Macdonald
### (2001–2004)
First show: Autumn/Winter 2001–2002 Couture
Collection, Paris, July 2001

# Riccardo Tisci
## (2005–2017)
First show: Autumn/Winter 2005–2006 Couture
Collection, Paris, July 2005

# Clare Waight Keller
## (2017–2020)
First show: Spring/Summer 2018 Couture Collection,
Paris, October 2017

# Matthew M. Williams
## (2020–2024)
First show: Spring/Summer 2022 Couture Collection,
Paris, October 2021

# Sarah Burton
## (2024–present)
First collection: Paris, March 2025

I'm not Givenchy. I'm Alexander McQueen.

**99**

### Alexander McQueen

An iconic design figure in his own right, chaffed against the expectations of a heritage haute couture house, haloscape.org, February 28, 2024

The creative directorship of Givenchy again made headlines in 2001 with the appointment of Welsh knitwear designer Julien Macdonald.

Unlike his predecessors, Macdonald was unafraid to turn to the archives for inspiration, drawing on Givenchy's love of clean lines, fur and even reimagining the "Bettina" blouse.

However, his collections failed to make a splash and his contract was terminated after two years.

Let's face it, I haven't had the greatest success there.

## Julien Macdonald

On his time at Givenchy, theguardian.com, January 22, 2004

My shoes are always high, my clothes always sparkle, and that's what I like. It's not going to be everybody's cup of tea. That's what I do. If you want conceptual fashion, or if you want something serious then you go to somebody else. But for me, clothes have always been about dressing up. They can lift your spirit and change your mood.

**Julien Macdonald**

Acknowledging his critics in a 2003 interview, *The Guardian*, September 7, 2003

The couture house then pinned its hopes on gothic Italian designer Riccardo Tisci.

By Autumn/Winter 2006, the fashion press had declared Tisci to be Givenchy's saviour, with his ability to balance that classic Parisienne Givenchy chic with more avant-garde gothic flair.

I love romanticism and sensuality, maybe because I come from a family with eight sisters.

**Riccardo Tisci**

Tisci's upbringing, much like Givenchy, was dominated by feminine energy, archive.nytimes.com, February 28, 2007

So, even though I had a fantastic family, surrounded with all these amazing women, I always felt lonely – not lonely in the melancholic way but knowing that, to really survive, I have to do everything for myself. I had to work and study, and I was out in the street really surviving, bringing food back home.

**Riccardo Tisci**

On his difficult upbringing, interviewmagazine.com, February 2, 2016

I'm also a person who is very
emotional. I like black; I like white.
I never like what's in the middle.
And the runway is where I try to
transmit this.

**Riccardo Tisci**

Often dismissing the categorization of his work as simply gothic,
archive.nytimes.com, February 28, 2007

"

The designer's preferred look, a strange and sexed-up romanticism, was established from his very first outing. From there, he's been able to play many variations on the theme, from drowned sailor goths, to tribal goths, to Catholic goths, to urban goths, to well, goth goths. It's not like he invented the colour but, thanks in no small part to Tisci, we've spent another good decade in black.

"

**Dazed magazine**

On Tisci's time at Givenchy, dazeddigital.com, February 3, 2017

Now I can give a beautiful present, and that may change the lives of people around me. But, still, anything I do, I do with my heart.

**Riccardo Tisci**

On his reputation for being quite an intense person to work with, interviewmagazine.com, February 2, 2016

As well as providing the label some much-needed stability throughout his twelve-year tenure, Riccardo Tisci also gave Givenchy several iconic fashion moments.

This included the Givenchy Spring/Summer 2015 Julia Roberts campaign where the actress was given the brief "no smile, no make-up" and the Autumn/Winter 2015 campaign featuring rival designer Donatella Versace.

I approached my friend Donatella because she represents what a fashion icon is to me. We thought it was time to break boundaries and give a strong message about how to think fashion.

**Riccardo Tisci**

On the decision to feature fellow designer Donatella Versace in the Givenchy Autumn/Winter 2015 campaign, dazeddigital.com, June 24, 2015

Tisci also brought many firsts to the House of Givenchy and to fashion as a whole.

A champion of diversity and inclusion, Tisci ensured that a range of ethnicities and backgrounds were represented on the catwalk, including the first transgender model to front a major haute couture campaign, Lea T.

People can be so avant-garde, so advanced, but actually not, because people are still making differences between skin colour.

**Riccardo Tisci**

On diversity in the fashion industry, dazeddigital.com, February 2, 2017

Riccardo is determined. He is a good human being. And he is never jealous. He has a great sense of humour. And is always telling terrible, dirty jokes.

**Marina Abramović**

Ballet dancer and long-time collaborator of Tisci's, Marina Abramović, on the designer's unique flair, dazeddigital.com, August 9, 2013

Hubert de Givenchy's confident style has always been an inspiration.

**Waight Keller**

Paying homage to Givenchy's founder, theguardian.com, March 16, 2017

I was inspired by romance.

**Riccardo Tisci**

On the driving force behind his designs, dazeddigital.com,
August 9, 2013

Tisci left fashionistas and critics alike stunned when he announced his move from Givenchy to Versace in 2017.

He left behind him a legacy of the man who righted the Givenchy ship after a turbulent period.

The next designer to step up to the mantle was former Chloé creative director Clare Waight Keller, the first woman to occupy the position of creative director.

True elegance comes with a natural gesture, an attitude in simplicity.

**Givenchy**

Announcing the appointment of Clare Waight Keller with the above quote on Instagram, along with an archival image of Givenchy, theguardian.com, March 16, 2017

" By that measure, however, while there was nothing in particular to object to – the collection was well-researched and polished, with a professional brief – there were also no new standards set, no landmark reinterpretations offered on the subject of identity and its expression. "

### *The New York Times*

A review of Clare Waight Keller's first Givenchy show, nytimes.com, October 1, 2017

**"**

# I'm so reckless when I rock my Givenchy dress.

**"**

Lyrics from Beyonce's 2016 chart-topping song
"Formation". The singer often worked closely with the House
of Givenchy and Riccardo Tisci, wmagazine.com,
February 6, 2016

While bringing elegant femininity back into Givenchy would be Waight Keller's lasting legacy, her best known design at Givenchy would be Meghan Markle's wedding dress for her royal wedding to Prince Harry in 2018.

The dress featured a bateau neckline, a creation of Hubert de Givenchy.

Don't *start* your business.
Go out there and learn in the
business.

**Waight Keller**

Sharing her advice for making it in the fashion industry,
vogue.com, January 14, 2019

Clare Waight Keller left Givenchy after "three wonderful years" in 2020. She was replaced by streetwear designer Matthew M. Williams.

A design legacy, Williams was more in line with the edgier street styles that Tisci brought into the house over Keller's elegant simplicity. Williams also made history as the first American in the role.

I want to make clothing that has emotions and soul and feels like it's been touched by the human hand, not that it's been spit out by a machine or a computer or something like that. I want these pieces to feel like they've been worked.

**99**

**Matthew M. Williams**

Speaking to *Vogue* in 2020 about his goal at Givenchy, vogue.com, October 7, 2020

66

You don't need Givenchy,
you need Jesus.

99

A lyric from international number one song "First Class"
by Jack Harlow, billboard.com, April 19, 2022

Very elegant and powerful
and chic.

**Matthew M. Williams**

Sharing his vision of the "Givenchy woman", vogue.com,
October 4, 2020

With his background in street wear and costume design for the likes of Lady Gaga and Kanye West, Williams' version of Givenchy was a big hit with the next generation of A-list celebrities such as Bella Hadid and Kendall and Kylie Jenner.

I am so excited to be able to write the next chapter in the story of this iconic house and to bring to Givenchy my own vision, sensibility and beliefs. **"**

**Sarah Burton**

On her appointment to Givenchy, wmagazine.com,
September 9, 2024

In 2020, the House of Givenchy was valued at US $2 billion, and estimates show that it has only continued to grow. Matthew M. Williams, tasked with translating Givenchy to Generation Z, raised eyebrows upon the announcement that he was leaving the fashion house in 2023.

His successor is Sarah Burton, formerly Alexander McQueen's right-hand woman.

You have to know when to stop – that's wisdom.

### Givenchy

Sharing parting words of advice, graciousquotes.com, December 1, 2023

Hubert de Givenchy's legacy is one of elegance, innovation and timeless beauty. Through decades of creativity and precision, Givenchy crafted pieces that transcend fashion, celebrating individuality and artistry.

His designs remain an enduring gift, a testament to his belief that style is not just about beauty, but an expression of soul.

It's a fabulous thing, to give life to fabric, to make something move well, the harmony of colour.

**Givenchy**

Independent.co.uk, June 7, 2010